Circumstances, Conundrums, and Commoners

Circumstances, Conundrums, and Commoners

T. C. Hood

Copyright © 2017 by T. C. Hood.

Library of Congress Control Number:		2017916487
ISBN:	Hardcover	978-1-5434-6102-2
	Softcover	978-1-5434-6103-9
	eBook	978-1-5434-6104-6

All rights reserved. No part of this book may be reproduced or transmitted in any form or by any means, electronic or mechanical, including photocopying, recording, or by any information storage and retrieval system, without permission in writing from the copyright owner.

Any people depicted in stock imagery provided by Thinkstock are models, and such images are being used for illustrative purposes only. Certain stock imagery © Thinkstock.

Print information available on the last page.

Rev. date: 11/11/2017

To order additional copies of this book, contact:
Xlibris
1-888-795-4274
www.Xlibris.com
Orders@Xlibris.com
760625

This book is dedicated to my father, Max Kay Hood who taught me that poetry is something to live, to share and to enjoy with others.

The image is fine.

A metaphor marvelous!

A simile analogous,

    suggesting the real..

But what could be better

than breaking word's fetter

and knowing in thoughts

    that we feel.

Table of Contents

Section One: Circumstances

1. Signs..3
2. The Snow Tree..5
3. Redbud Tree...7
4. The Singing Forest..9
5. Forgotten Flowers...11
6. Blaze...13
7. Moon Mirror...15
8. The tangled web..17
9. A view from the choir...19
10. Graffiti..21

Section Two: Connundrums

1. Fading to Blank..25
2. A Bushel of Apples...27
3. Strawberry Picking...29
4. Neutron Bomb..31
5. The Blindfold..33
6. Termites..35
7. Struggle...37
8. I am America, weeping...39
9. Calloused Consciences...41
10. Young At Heart...43

Section Three: Commoners

1. Dwight 47
2. Miss Hazel 49
3. Caring 51
4. The Difference 53
5. In As Much… 55
6. Bound for Glory 59
7. Life and death are full of mystery 61
8. Friendship 63
9. I AM 65
10. What Shall We Say 67
11. The Logic of Love 69
12. I've Grown Accustomed to my Fat 71

Section One: Circumstances

SIGNS

COLD BEEEE

R   OPEN

said the litany on

a sign

>-----------------------------------→

HERE.

Pointers
     grab
          my socketed eyes,

Wrenching
     my attention from the hammerlock of mind.

Why?   When it's dark flourescent night---

Late walking the street----

Are signs so many ;

people so few??

The Snow Tree

The snow tree rests silently
 in the morning mist,
Swaying its feathered branches
carelessly on the wasting wind.

The storm has been here
Bending each pine's reach
toward the source of storms.

Now the forest waits
Like a huge flock of brood hens
protecting with their wings
the roots of life to come.

Redbud Tree

Redbud blossoms soft,
 Pink clusters on ebony limbs.

You simple scrag tree---
Gnarled and bent, I know you
 by the spring wind blowing
 your pink confetti through my garden.

Companion of the dogwood,
You glow irridescent
 in your bare indecency
  and warm spring sunlight.

In summer I almost missed you
Modestly cloaked in forest green
 your seed pods dangling
 like some overgrown, unkempt shrub.

But last December, I saw you
 huddled on the hillside,
 bent over our still-green holly
 as if to warm your cold gray branches in its life.

Now blossoms burst from warmth
 cluster to proclaim your glory quietly.
Spring captures me again
 with sudden beauty.

The Singing Forest

Each trunk and leaf whispers to me
My spirit's fingers trace the giggling leaves
My tears form little rivers through bark canyons.
My eyes blink as they cross the slanting shafts of sunlight
   descending through the gloom from high above me.

Walking through the forest, my mind
   wanders backward to beginnings..
Seeds of mighty giants are reborn.
Stumps like blackened stubble
   rot scattered among thin new trees.

I could and did get lost in forests--
   during childhood in my grandfather's woodlot.
The forest floor was green with May apples,
Dutchmen's britches, Bloodroot
   and nameless wild flowers....

Gardens are so civilized!
Gravel paths and bedded plantings-
Pink petunias and purple pansies—
Oh! Gardens are the handiwork of gardeners!
The forest is the jungle---still untamed.
The tangle of the undergrowth provides
   a challenge, a path to clear or just to find.
Small furry creatures blur by me.
The birds perched high above me

call to each other while
The forest and I sing softly to ourselves..
Regardless of the season,
   we are one!

Forgotten Flowers of the Field

Lest you should think with too much pride
 about achievements strong and brave;
Your name called "Great" now...far and wide
Shall be forgotten in the grave.

Yet memories of lively days
  will replay in the minds of those
  who carry on in work and play
The fragrant beauty of the rose.

Flowers flourish in the field;
Grass grows green and trees stand firm.
Flesh and blood will always yield—
  unless sustained by love returned.

God's steadfast love does all inspire
An outpouring of mercy, grace.
"Forgiveness!" sings the angel choir,
Salvation for the human race.

Blaze

See the fire.
Triangles of multi-colored light
Leap through the cracks
Bending around each log
Flying above the mottled, blinking glow,
In the skeleton of the grate.
Shimmering vapors turn to smoke.

Hear the fire.
A warm crackling song
Above softly falling drifts of gray ashes
The fire hisses, pops
As simmering, steam removes dampness
Still lingering in the rain-wet wood.

Feel the fire.
The red-orange tongues
Licking the bone cold seeps through muscle-
The heat caresses skin
Like some forgotten stray, who in a thoughtful moment
Warmed your hand.

Taste the fire.
Swallowing the smoke
Whose flavor recalls ham and cheddar cheese
Or burnt marshmallows toasted on a stick
Last summer over a grateless blaze.

Memories reside in the gods' gift to humankind.

Moon Mirror

The moon is the sun's looking glass
  against the black of space
We see reflected back and down
  men's memories of day past.

But when there's snow, the light
  Reflected back and up
Becomes the moon's reflection of the sun
  On earth—or whose or what? Or where?

Where is light possessed – caught and held—
  Except within the eye of man or beast
Or in the bloom of flowers?
And yet, we may be mirrors
For light passing through
  Between life and life.
You or I may be caught in glancing smiles
Until one single beam may gather; fire out
  Pulsating in infinite regress
Light penetrates the furthest dim recess
  Of our universe.

The tangled web

No spider's web that I have seen
hangs tangled—drifting in a breeze
Unless some human hand has torn
  its symetery in strands.

Humans weave the tangled webs
  made from half-truths and lies,
  flattering some while pleasing none,
making and breaking ties.

Friendships endure beyond the bonds
contracts create with words.
The healing touch of sisterhood
  transcends life's milling herds.

From cattle calls for extras
to noisy union halls,
We see what our professions allow
when gathered with our pals.

Day in, day out words echo on
'til reaching printer's web,
Dispute, conjecture, wit and poem
in ink our voices ebb.

So quickly and so quietly
  these tangled webs decay.
The pages burn with captured fire---
  words cry, then fade away.

A view from the choir

The upturned faces of the congregation
Are stained yellow, violet, blue from the sunlight
streaming through high windows,
  portraits of prophets and apostles in vivid purple,
red, orange.
Attentive listeners among the drooping heads of
meditative sleepers
  provide unintended canvas for the hues from the
stained glass scenes.

As the sun shifts, different well-scrubbed faces are
highlighted.
White shirts catch the light and dark coats absorb it.
Some sit in shadows while light kisses others.
The message makes no distinction –
amplified equally for the stopped, ringing and eager
ears of all within the cathedral.
Will it sounds be heard?
Will the words be recognized as sentences?
Will the spoken sentences yield meaning?

The sun moves on!
Incandescent illumination lights the nave.
The worship ends
The sanctuary quiets gradually as the last notes of
the postlude fade into memory.
Voices greet and take leave in familiar tones.

As the sounds of worship turn to silence---
Sunshine and sermon seem caught within walls of cold stone and empty benches.
The people depart.
Has the light through prophets stained their souls?
Will their faces witness the joy of inspiration and renewal?
Can their tongues proclaim God's majesty?
Will they dare to do His love?

Graffiti

Privacy inspires defacement
Limericks engraved on wood, marble, metal—
Are these words or drawings?
Outpourings of the quiet concentration
  Inspired by concentration
  Or even masturbation??

Alone yet present in a public place
Sounds of nearby others
Relieving themselves of bodily excretions
Would not seem likely to inspire.

Library restrooms may be candidates
 Scratched out instructions for a sexual tryst
Or commentary on current political leadership
Or even on the character of the readership..

Now if the sounds of "other" come with groans
Or if the sound of "others" seem quite strange,
Does the need for commentary provoke
A line or two of prose or verse?
Or just an exclamation!

Graffiti! Is it more than "breaking wind"?
A passing moment enclosed silence inspires?
Boxed in with just "one's self"
  Perhaps just casual comments
  On some obsenity of life.

Section Two: Connundrums

Fading to Blank

Shades of gray populate the garden furnitured pool room.
With the ever present TV, I enter --- a voice,
  an image flickering in the bright sun, against the shades of gray,
I fade   into the flowered wallpaper of nowhere.

She speaks,
I know these strangers. They've come a long way to see me.
What are their names?
Oh! The blackness and the cold! Wandering lost in the dark,
Darling! Where are you? Where are you?
I've found a haven, by myself, by myself, by myself.
I've found a haven. Darling! Where are you?
No! You say you brought me here.
Darling! I want to go home!
I'm a big girl! Now. I can, will take care of myself.
Next week. Next week. Next week. I'll go home.
Progress.
Did you know I'm going to work again?
Yes, I need a job. Typing, a good secretary. I have good skills.
Love! But I can't go home until we do something about the stairwells.
Falling down stair wells would be dangerous.
We don't have stairwells you say!
You know, sometimes people tell me things I know aren't true.
But I pretend to agree, to know just to please them.
How can they know?
Can they know?
They know....they know.

Another speaks,
Have you got a light, Sir?
No! Son, ask the man.
Have you got a a light Sir? Have you got a light, sir? I have a cigarette...

She speaks,
Cranberry juice, you say.
Cranberry juice for old folks.
Cranberry jooose for strokes.

Gray shades populate the garden furnitured pool room.
The images flicker on the ever present television.
I leave as I came a voice, an image black in the bright sun.
Amidst the shades of gray, I fade into the flowered wallpaper of nowhere.

A Bushel of Apples

I don't know how many years they've come out to the farm.

"Helena, Helena---The Smiths are here for their Spies. Come
out and say hello!"

Must be fifteen, twenty years ago,
they started driving up from Elkhart.
The same every year. Three bushels of Spies
and a bushel of Romes.

"The apples look good this year, Max."

Yes, they look good. A good year---
but they've come every year good and bad.
Faithful customers, friends--
a man can build on that.

"Here's another box to fill."

Every year the same sturdy cardboard boxes
to fill with firm, fresh apples.
Roll them in gently so they won't bruise.!
Be sure to give full measure!

"There's a few more for the top to round it off."

Something about a bright ripe apple in your hand,
Especially when you've help it grow.
The noisy, moist crunch as your teeth break its flesh
or when Helena's baking apple pie
The tart shimmering cinnamon scent
that tempts your tongue to taste.

"These spies will make good pies."

How many times have I said that and Harry Smith
and Joan chuckled at the rhyme?
Well, time to say good-bye;
To take the check or change the bill.

"Thanks Harry. See you next year."

Gosh, Harry's getting gray.

"Good to see you, Joan.   Come back again."

Come back again. A bushel of apples is more
than a trip to the country.

Strawberry Picking

>   I

A field of strawberries
lost in that summer time of freedom
after college.
A frozen moment suspended
  before marriage and more study.

Who was I then -- watching the pickers
   bending toward the earth
   searching for the berries?

A dirty, khaki-clad migrant father sees
     the boss' son. ("Hi, boss! A smile for your son whose
supervisin'---
    What else do bosses' sons do? Nothin'. ")

Gladys, a neighbor, working in the packing shed
   her different time caught
   bound in past musings....
A small boy stopping in for cookies--- "How could he be
   out of college now and getting---   married?!!"

Time runs fast for neighbors watching children.
Time drifts slowly past for migrant workers.

II
Gladys wonders and my thoughts seem
   as far away from these home fields
   as the clumping rain clouds.
Their thunder and grayness bring cool respite
   from the sun-baked search for berries.
"How many beeries in a box to earn a penny?
   And if you have to pull their caps for freezin'
    How many boxes make a dollar?
     or bread to fill the children
      or a bottle to find a spirit
lost in the green mazes,
wandering in silent search for berries."

My Mom spoons strawberries on cottage cheese and cautions me,
   "Son, you can't be picker and boss together."

III
Perhaps you think of strawberries with shortcake
Of summer parties' fun and cake and ice cream,
Frolicking feet on a carpet of green
A carefree breeze and swinging hair.

Pain plates the berries, I remember,
Tatters for clothes, sun-burned nose
Strained back and aching brain.
Grim reflections dim the supermarket luster.
Reclaim that box of berries---empty.

Comes the unspoken refrain--
"Dim the sun!
Cloud the sky!
Bring the wind!
And rain, rain.....

NEUTRON BOMB

A NEUTRON BOMB LANDED QUIETLY ON OUR CAMPUS.
LAUNCHED FROM A HIGH PLACE BY THE SYSTEM WITH A TRIGGERING DEVICE DESIGNED BY ADMINISTRATIVE FORCES
A NEUTRON BOMB LANDED ON OUR CAMPUS.

ONE BY ONE STUDENTS AND FACULTY STARTED FALLING
DEAD... ON THE COOL SPRING GREEN LAWNS
DEAD AT A LECTERN IN THE CLASSROOMS
DEAD BENT OVER A MICROSCOPE IN A LABORATORY
DEAD IN A THE MIDDLE OF DRESS REHEARSAL
DEAD HAND STILL ON THE KEYBOARD
DEAD IN GYMNASIUM AND SWIMMING POOL
THE CAMPUS GREW VERY SILENT.

PEOPLE ARRIVED FROM ACROSS THE STATE
  AND EVEN FROM OUTSIDE THE COUNTRY
WEARING THOSE BULKY SUITS THAT PROTECT YOU FROM
  DEADLY RADIATION
THEY CAME TO RECOVER THE BODIES OF SONS, DAUGHTERS,
    SISTERS, BROTHERS, HUSBANDS, WIVES, UNCLES, AUNTS,
  GRANDMOTHERS, GRANDFATHERS.
THEY TOOK THE BODIES AWAY.
A MEMORIAL PLAQUE WAS PLACED.

LIFE HUMMED BUSILY INSIDE THE SHIELDED TOWER OF ADMINISTRATION.... THIRTY-FOOT-THICK, TEN STORIES TALL
SLABS OF LEAD—KEPT THE NEUTRONS OUT OF THE NERVE CENTER
OF CAMPUS ACTIVITY

KEPT THE NEWS OUT.
KEPT THE VIEWS OUT OF A DYING LEARNING COMMUNITY.

NEVERTHELESS. THE LIGHTS STAYED ON. THE TOILETS FLUSHED.
ELEVATORS OPERATED UP AND DOWN.
AIR CONDITIONERS COOLED AND FURNACES HEATED.
EVEN THE BOOKS IN THE LIBRARY WERE UNHARMED ...
ON THE DAY THE NEUTRON BOMB LANDED ON OUR CAMPUS.

SOMETIME AFTER THE NEUTRON BOMB LANDED ON OUR CAMPUS
AN INSPECTION TOUR WAS HELD.
A HELIOCOPTER CARRYING THE GOVERNOR, LEGISLATORS, TRUSTEES AND PRESDIENT OF THE SCHOOL FLEW OVER THE SCENE.
THEY MARVELED AT THE TIDINES OF THE PLACE.
THE COMMENTED ON THE FINE NEW BUILDINGS.
THE COMPLIMENTED THE INVENTORY OF EQUIPMENT AND LIBRARY HOLDINGS.
THEY COMMENDED THE PRESIDENT ON THE FACT THAT
NO COMPLAINTS HAD BEEN RECEIVED FROM FACULTY OR STUDENTS.

A NEUTRON BOMB LANDED ON OUR CAMPUS.
IT KILLED ALL THE FACULTY AND STUDENTS.
IS A UNIVERSITY MORE THAN ITS FACILITIES?

The Blindfold

Consider the statue of a woman
Clothed in flowing gown
Her outstretched arm holds a balance—
 a way to compare the weight of two objects.

The woman's face is comely.
Around her head a cloth is tied
Covering both her eyes.
She cannot see the way the balance tiips.

I have heard that this statue is the artist's idea of the old saying ----
"justice is blind." This is not the voluntary blindness of love!
This blindness is enforced.
Who placed the blindfold on this silent lady?
What does that wretched folded cloth foretell?

Do images deceive more quickly than do words?
Who claims that one picture is worth one thousand words?
Words move slowly as they assault our minds!
Perhaps the weight of arguments can be observed, when balanced against others.
But images, images, images can they be weighted?

Images are like music---I can feel them.
Images can be described in words, but some verbal traslations remove what certainty was there before...
I want to say that images create a passion to convict—
To make a judgment as to who is right or wrong.
Eye witnesses testify with certainty.
Radical makeovers suggest that you should only believe half of what you see!
Should eye witnesses be required to wear blindfolds too?

Wouldn't that make their testimony more convincing.
Does blindness to the moment symbolize neutrality?
Our world is full of images today.
Our world is full of words that represent.
Our world is full of manufactured faces—
 posed and retouched photos—purposeful propaganda.

I cannot tell a lie. My lips are sealed in silent testimony.

Termites

Termites will eat your house,
 They come!
Leave you standing without a home.
There you are!
Naked, alone!
No solid board to call your own.
Abandoned! Abandoned!

A suburban skeleton standing there,
With broken glass, half-eaten chairs,
Tangled draperies, rustling the air,
Neighbors smirking behind their stares.
Scorned! Scorned!

All because you failed to see
The termites swarming around your trees
Nor paid the exterminator inspection fee
To come and say, "Oh, Mercy me!"
Forgotten! Forgotten!

Such are the times of suburban bliss
When no neighbor cares a bad damn piss
Unless your house is better than hiss
And your name appears on a better list.
Hated! Hated!

Oh! The termites they come and the termites
   they go.
Maybe they'll wait for a year or so
To fill their bellies with another's hole--
And the mice they come and the mice they go
Blinded! Blinded!

Struggle

A giant stirs from slumber in the South.
Pure words in honeyed voices fail to form.
The children born at Babel stay forlorn.
Pride stalks, the strutter, the dark behemoth.

The silent symbol of a surface world--
The quiet, callous calm, these hundred years
Cast singing warriors whom the lynch mob fears
Unrecognized, behind black faces blurred.

Old hatreds flicker in the cross-bright flames.
Where are the words that two men spoke as one?
Loud horns cry out while wealth divides the tongue,
And men call color scores of other names.

Trembling now, we stand in worlds we dreamed--
You and Yours in some uncharted world.
Cross and crown, the banners are unfurled.
New earth is born amidst the hymns and screams.

I am America, weeping..

I feel America fading,
a country once borne strong
out of the womb of revolutionary courage.
The First New Nation
Free from the heritage of monarchy
not owing to any particular religious tradition.
Declaring itself under God but not requiring
allegiance to any well-turned out theology.

Now a too ripe apple, America
rots in a surfeit of pleasure,
an affluent society that has lost the edge
provided by expanding frontiers.
Too much dulls the consciousness.
Moral leadership decays
jaded by old knowledge and
new compromises taken to "close the deal."

I see America falling,
tuning inward---only to find
an empty heart beating to an economy
tuned to lust, carnal delights, once surpressed
become the only source of new passion
for .... freedom? Legacy of the sixties,
The word sticks in my throat.
For I am America and I weep---
perhaps, the last tears of hope.

Calloused   Consciences

Remember America agonized
like the some gigantic Lincoln
Bent with sun-browned face lined with concern
 pursuing justice, striding slowly forward through
winds of change.

No! Not that vision
America—a stone cold monument
A failed republic long ago frozen
Hard and unrelenting
Cracking, instead of yielding to
 pain, proverty, pressure of protest and

How easily we think about the multitude
experiencing poverty or pain.
Our news magazines and papers report injuries to the poor
Immigrants choosing to leave rather than be deported
Next to advertisements for Vacations in Jamaica and luxury cars
Consecutive pages of our reading material
Stories of environmental degradation lay open
On beautifully crafted tables
in upholstery insulated "living rooms".

An easily overlooked aspect
Of the electronic miracles of television, internet, radio
access to information bringing humans close ---
into a worldwide tribe—
the well-cushioned coffin of the easy chair dims our vision.

Closeness in this context breeds the callousness
  Of too easily won familiarity
No pain born of black, brown or red skin

No blood, no empty stomach
  fighting a illness you can't afford..
just a brief glimpse through an electronic window at
  lives beyond the barrier of leisure
An experience, a late movie---perhaps, a half-waking dream.
A little like reading the impassioned commentary by radicals,
  who would rather rant than act.

I have seen your documentaries America.
  Financed by companies who'd rather reveal the problems
  they created than work to solve them
    -----and thus through an implicit, contrite confession
    purge themselves of guilt...
Listening to the chorus of our voices chanting.
"Oh! How awful!" "Oh! How true!"

Beating on our breasts and doing nothing..

God.

I wonder what a nation of white-washed tombs
would look like?
White-washed tombs instead of people ...
I guess there wouldn't be eyes to see.
Or ears to hear the poison wind whispering among the tombs.
"Oh! How awful!"
"Oh! How true!"

Young At Heart

As my Father grew older he had several favorite songs.
One was from the movie version of the Mary Poppins stories.
"Let's go fly a kite…"
I remember times when I was very young that we flew
Or tried to fly a kite together.
No fancy kite but definitely one with a tail made of cloth and rags.

And it was my Father who taught me to play
"knife baseball" with a jack knife and a piece of old lumber.
My uncles were the ones who took me fishing
But my Father was our club's 4-H Leader in charge.

Perhaps his favorite song was one recorded by the
Venerable Jimmy Durante. In his raspy voice
He sang… "Don't you know that it's worth
Every treasure on earth
To be Young at Heart…"

Clearly- a man who could simply enjoy looking
At the golden glow of a peach in this hand at sunset
Was young at heart..
His heart was the that of a poet
And a song was often in his head if not on his lips…

Like Will Rogers, one of his heroes, he never met a man
He didn't like.
He loved life but did not fear death
He told me not long before he died in his sleep..
That he thought he had finished writing his memoir…
He was truly and forever will be young at heart.

Section Three: Commoners

FOR DWIGHT

IN KNOXVILLE A MAN NAMED DWIGHT
LOOKED AROUND FOR THE VERY BEST LIGHT
"LUMINESCENCE," SAID HE, "PROVIDES JUST THE RIGHT KEY
TO PAINT A YOUNG NUDE IN MY SIGHT."

FOR MANY YEARS PAST, DWIGHT'S WORKPLACE TASK
WAS FRAMING LIFE'S STRUGGLES IN WORDS.
BUT AS WORDS GREW STALE AND BRUSH STROKES GREW BOLD
PICTURES CAPTURED YOUNG BEAUTIES UNTOLD.

BIRTHDAYS ROLLED ON BY!
WHILE SONGS FILLED OUR HEARTS,
THE MUSIC PLAYED ON IN OUR SOULS.
PAINTINGS EXPRESSED WHERE WORDS FAILED TO TELL;
GESTURES AND COLOR MADE WHOLE.

WE TASTE, HEAR SMELL, SEE
FIND DIALOGUE, SKETCHES OR PHRASE.
FULFILLMENT IN LIFE COMES TO EACH ONE
AS FRIENDS SHARE THE FEELINGS OF GRACE.

Miss Hazel

That's how she was known at the church.
I visited her later in her home, but that isn't how I met her.
I met Miss Hazel first through the eyes of a little girl.
It was our first Sunday visiting a new church. Our old church had simply decided
   to disband in failure to achieve its suburban and intellectual potential. Members were each
   choosing a way to go. They were finding their way to other congregations in the city.
We found our way to Vestal United Methodist and Miss Hazel.

Like many other Sunday School Teachers, Miss Hazel loved every new child.
Miss Hazel showed that love with flowers from those she grew in her yard.
Particularly on that first Sunday, I can see in my memory's eye a small bouquet.
Perhaps five or six stems of flowers (Was there a wet paper towel around them
 to keep them moist?) clutched in one hand of our four-year-old daughter, Heather.
The smile on her lips and in her eyes told of the happiness and acceptance she had
received that morning.
We Learned later that this happened often as Miss Hazel brought flowers from her
garden to the students in her classes.

I grew up in the Methodist Church.
My Sunday School Teachers had given me many things, including a lasting
foundation --- both emotional and rational –in the faith. But no Sunday School Teacher

had ever given me flowers. But Miss Hazel gave this first-time visitor to her class
a handful of love in color and scent—flowers.

Miss Hazel taught Sunday School at Vestal for over forty years, until she could no
longer do it due to declining vigor and advancing age. But Miss Hazel will live on
beyond her ninety-one years on this earth –in her many small acts of kindness that
inspired faith in children. The children and their parents remember and are
glad for her witness to the joy of life with God.

Let us celebrate the goodness of Miss Hazel Doyle Endsley's life.

Miss Hazel

That's how she was known at the church.
I visited her later in her home, but that isn't how I met her.
I met Miss Hazel first through the eyes of a little girl.
It was our first Sunday visiting a new church. Our old church had simply decided
   to disband in failure to achieve its suburban and intellectual potential. Members were each
   choosing a way to go. They were finding their way to other congregations in the city.
We found our way to Vestal United Methodist and Miss Hazel.

Like many other Sunday School Teachers, Miss Hazel loved every new child.
Miss Hazel showed that love with flowers from those she grew in her yard.
Particularly on that first Sunday, I can see in my memory's eye a small bouquet.
Perhaps five or six stems of flowers (Was there a wet paper towel around them
   to keep them moist?) clutched in one hand of our four-year-old daughter, Heather.
The smile on her lips and in her eyes told of the happiness and acceptance she had
received that morning.
We Learned later that this happened often as Miss Hazel brought flowers from her
garden to the students in her classes.

I grew up in the Methodist Church.
My Sunday School Teachers had given me many things, including a lasting
foundation --- both emotional and rational –in the faith. But no Sunday School Teacher

had ever given me flowers. But Miss Hazel gave this first-time visitor to her class
a handful of love in color and scent—flowers.

Miss Hazel taught Sunday School at Vestal for over forty years, until she could no
longer do it due to declining vigor and advancing age. But Miss Hazel will live on
beyond her ninety-one years on this earth –in her many small acts of kindness that
inspired faith in children. The children and their parents remember and are
glad for her witness to the joy of life with God.

Let us celebrate the goodness of Miss Hazel Doyle Endsley's life.

Caring

The lightest brush of lip with lip
The softest touch of fingertips
The whispered songs we often share
These are the signs you care.

The children's portraits on the wall
The desk set cracked once from a fall
The well-thumbed Bibles we consume
Tell of our ways of love.

Chipped wedding plates of thirty years
Teenagers grown through world-wide fears
Ceramic wish box, books, dulcimer
These things furnish our home.

What memories will make us old?
Will we re-live the tales we've told?
No! Each day brings some new, strange road
That brings us close to God.

Wet snow, blue grass, salt sweat, gray bees
Song birds, orange skies, chapped skin, oak trees
Lives grown entwined like ivy leaves
Environments we share.

Dare still to care
With each new day
Until we both shall
Pass away.

The Difference

Clothes make the man!
What makes a woman?
Language, the cosmetologist?
Some designing man?
These words cannot explain
failures of men to understand women.
or errors of women who try to understand men.

Does woman make man?
Of course!
We understand the womb that woman carries—
  the dark and hidden place where bodies grow—
  at least until that moment
  of anguished separation
  called birth—
When once what was part of me
 Becomes another.

I am a man.
My contribution was out of pleasure.
I gave the sperm gladly.
I enjoyed the moment.
I did not carry with me
  the growing sense of other.
I did not feel my breasts swell with milk for life.
I did not grow weary of the water cushioning a flesh
  becoming not my own.
I did not strain through hours of labor to hear
  that glorious first cry.

Perhaps the difference is:
  Women suffer pain
   to bring new life
 While men
   just pleasure in love
  and wonder what suffering is about...

In As Much...

Where does God live?
The thoughtful person asked.
Caught in a time when past assurances
Remained silent...
It seemed that God was dead!

Losses, daily troubles
Surrounded this question, which seemed
More like a desperate cry,
Seeking to restore
The hope that once
Shown forth so easily
In the minutia of life.

Does God live at all?
Even the bright sunlight,
The comfort of friends
Could not silence
The ever-present doubt
Choking the life out
Of the faith that once lived there.

Words are hollow reminders
Of the absence of belief.
How could people be so unkind?
If God exists,
Why does war and want continue?
How can God be
Amidst such inequality
Such nastiness?

Exiled from God's presence
I cannot love to sing
The songs of Joy, of Hope
Of eternal Love.

Where does God exist?
 God exists in moments
Of shared concern
Of reaching across the vast gulf
That separates each soul.

Recognize that in the fleeting moment
When one soul touches another
The mystery
That is God
Exists for eternity.

Not in life as we know it
But in life as we are known
In life as we have been known
In life as we shall be known.

And so God exists in those eternal moments
And God remembers even when we forget
Those moments when
Soul touches Soul.

Bound for Glory

Woody Guthrie was my kind of man.
He was a minstrel.
I'd be like that too.

Jesus Christ was my kind of man.
He was a teacher.
I'd be like that too.

Mark Twain was my kind of man.
He saw "through" people.
I'd see through them too.

Martin Luther was my kind of man.
He was stubborn.
I'd be stubborn too.

M. Gandhi was my kind of man.
He loved peace.
I'd show that love too.

Oh! I'll sing you a song
And I'll sing it again
About people who knew
The where and the when
The how and the why
But before I go on
Remember that you've got
To write your own song.

To sing each day
Un-til you die
And then you'll sing it
Somewhere in the sky
Or where ever your road
to glory goes on
Past people and places
Each singing their song.

Life and death are full of mystery.

God created man.
So man created God
to understand the why of life.

But man still failed to understand
how to live And...
since God was conceived to be more knowledgeable, and powerful than man..
God needed to become man
To show man how to live.

Why not? The very idea seems improbable but then...
Intelligent life seems rather improbable,
in the overall scheme of "things" ---That are!!

But if God becomes man such an event threatens
The far off and above all image of a creator.
God becomes too approachable.
Therefore God as man must die in order to keep a believeable idea of God.
Of course, if God dies then God is not an example of infinite life. Unless....
The God become Man rises from the dead.

That makes God----God again.

So how is man supposed to live---Man is supposed to exemplify the love
 that God as man exemplified.
"Greater love hath no man than this---
that a man lays down his life for a friend."

If you can die for a friend, you know how to live???

Life and Death are full of mystery!!!

"Friendship"

I love you, not only for what you are,
but for what I am when I am with you.
I love you, not only for what you have made
of yourself, but for what you are making of me.
I love you for the part of me you bring out.
I love you for putting your hand into my heaped up
heart and passing over all the frivolous and weak things
you cannot help seeing there, and drawing out into the light
all the
beautiful and radiant things that no one else has looked quite
deep enough to find.
I love you for ignoring the possibilities of the fool in me, and
for laying firm hold of the possibilities of good in me.
I love you because you are helping me to make of the lumber
of my life
----not a tavern ---but a temple for God; and of the words of
my every day
---not reproach---but a song to Him.
I love you because you have done more than any creed
could have done to make me happy.
You have done it without a touch, without a sign—you
have done it by just being yourself.
After all, perhaps this is what being a real friend really means.

I AM

A momentary glimpse of truth

Lies hidden in the dark of an unconscious, notwillingtobefound

    corner

of   Each of us
    so

WHAT

ENTITLES Another to lead blindly groping, stumbling in

on a lot of old, lost memories of things forgotten

usefully, perhaps ----

         to stir us to recognize
ourselves

   for what we are

REALLY

NOW;

Don't you think Dr. Jones master of

Free associating, free will, free wheeling interdenominational

unaffiliated objective scientific advice that

INSIGHT

into self lies in voluntarily impudently making the realization

leap-of-faith assertion,

        "i   AM what I am !"   ?

What Shall We Say

What shall we say when we grow old,
And no one remembers the victories of youth,
When no one remembers the times we spoke truth?
What shall we say then?

What shall we say when we grow weak
And no one remembers the strength of our hands,
When our clenched fist could turn rocks into sand?
What shall we say then?

What shall we say when vision fades
And no one remembers the eyes that could see
Orange leaves, blue-sky water and wrens flying free?
What shall we say then?

What shall we say when we grow ill
And no one remembers the bed-ridden man
Dependent on nurses for food and bed-pan?
What shall we say then?

What shall we say when we can't speak?
Words will not form; thoughts merely pass.
Mind withers slowly beyond others grasp.
What shall we say then?

We shall say then that God endures!
Faith sustains hope and love will prevail!
Light streams through curtain shielding death's vale!
We shall pray then!

The Logic of Love

The people whom words cannot contain
Force arguments about their acts
Which seem both elegantly good and
Damnably arrogant, perhaps absurd,
or intentionally evil .

Too often, knowing motives
 is confused with knowing men.
And men for all seasons
often have mixed motives,
which baffle simpler minds
to whom choices seem so easy----
like black—white, day—night, right—wrong,
true—false, other ways
without a middle or a "sometimes."

I often wish I didn't see
the merit in other men's view.
Could stand firm with unquestioning mind,
Could be prejudiced and blind,
but then I think,
NO. It's better to say "maybe"
and not be so sure
for a while any way to love my enemy –
to see his path plainly—
to understand him.

It doesn't make sense
Even to me always---
But such is the logic of love.

I've Grown Accustomed to my Fat – A parody
   by Mary Lois Hood Ketchersid and Thomas Charles Hood

Verse One:
I've grown accustomed to my fat
It almost makes the day begin
I've grown accustomed to the meals
I eat each night and noon
Potatoes and eggs, bread pudding and steaks
They're second nature to me now
Like chewing up and swallowing down
I was once serenely skinny
And content with cottage cheese
Now I'm fat and happy
Just eating what I please
I've grown accustomed to the tremor
When I walk into a room
Accustomed to my fat.

Verse Two:
I've grown accustomed to my fat
I like its jiggle when I walk
I've grown accustomed to the stares
When I walk down the street
The comments, the jeers, the laughter, the tears
I'm well adapted to them now
Like the shouting out, "Hey you!"
I was once somewhat embarrassed
And would run away and hide
Now I face them bravely in my size eighty-fives.
I've grown accustomed to the roar
Of laughter behind my back---
Accustomed to my fat.

Verse Three:
I've grown accustomed to my fat
Why should I bother to reduce?
I've grown accustomed to the rolls that ooze over my belt
My jowls, my hips, my fifteen double chins
Are so familiar to me now.
They are my massive every day.
They fill each mirror fully,
As I am strolling by
If I again were thinner
I would not recognize "I."
I've grown accustomed to the clunk
When I step upon the scales.
Accustomed to my fat.

Verse Four:
I've grown accustomed to my fat
Its second-nature as they say
I've grown accustomed to the roll
That magnifies my waist
The fuss tailors make
When my measurements they take
Are very common to me now
Like struggling out and struggling in
I was once so slim and supple
My clothes were the right kind.
Now my fat hangs in folds in front
And pleats in my behind.
I'm just a mobile tent as I go down the street
Looking for my feet.

Verse Five
I've grown accustomed to my fat
I huff and puff, when I climb stairs
I've grown accustomed to the state of being short of breath
The throbbing, the pain, it's all just the same.
I'm well accustomed to them now
And doctors' warnings not aside
I take them all so bravely
Even though my stomach shakes
My blood pressure goes sky high
While my colon quakes
I've grown accustomed to prescriptions, diets, even threats.
Accustomed to my fat.

Finale
I've grown accustomed to my fat
So please don't ask me to reduce
It's really something special to be as big as me
For even in a crowd of people I am all you see
I've grown accustomed to the need
For larger bottomed chairs
Accustomed to my Fat.

Printed in the United States
By Bookmasters